DIGGING DEEPER

Mining Your Potential

Michael C. Young

with Michael Nicloy

Digging Deeper
Author: Michael C. Young
Contributing Author: Michael Nicloy
Contributing Editor: Amy Oaks
Cover Design & Interior Layout: Michael Nicloy

Author photos: Kimberly Laberge, Dan Zarwell
All other photos courtesy of Michael C. Young

Published by Reji Laberje Writing and Publishing
Quantity order requests can be emailed to:
publishing@rejilaberje.com

writing and Publishing
www.rejilaberje.com

ISBN: 1945907010
ISBN-13: 978-1945907012

BISAC Codes:

BUS041000 BUSINESS & ECONOMICS / Management
BUS106000 BUSINESS & ECONOMICS / Mentoring & Coaching
BUS087000 BUSINESS & ECONOMICS / Production & Operations Management

Digging Deeper is a Reji Laberje Writing and Publishing interactive text. More information about Mike Young and his book can be found on our Electronic Resource Hub (ERH), which can be accessed by the QR code below.

Find a free QR scanner for your smart device via a search through your device's app store, then scan the QR code with your smart device:

http://www.rejilaberje.com/mike-young.html

I dedicate this book to my wife of 52 years. She has followed me (sometimes kicking and screaming) through several major moves as my career demanded. To be in mining one has to be a bit of a vagabond, where home is where you are. My wife is naturally a "nester" and a home is more of a sanctuary. She nonetheless stuck with me through it all.

TABLE OF CONTENTS

FOREWORD

I have had both the pleasure and challenge of knowing the author, Michael Young, for more than thirty years. I worked under his management two levels down, directly for him and, in later years, as a peer on several projects. His techniques brought out my best performance in every instance. As a result, my skills developed over time allowing my career to advance along the journey. Therein, lies the pleasure and the challenge.

I worked for Mike for several years during the growth phase of my career. He applied the management concepts outlined in this book to me and other managers under his direction. I watched intently his balancing the strengths and weaknesses of the various teams under his leadership. He impressed me many times by reshuffling the players; resulting in a stronger team each time.

As outlined in *Digging Deeper*, one must accept the challenge to relocate to gain new levels of responsibility. Your career may advance to a certain level locally, but at a much slower pace due to limited opportunities, and it will, most likely, peak before reaching the upper levels of the corporate structure where the significant decisions are made. This is my personal experience and is confirmed by many Board Directors I serve with who have shared their many relocation stories as they advanced up the chain of command. These relocations have positive impacts on your life and career, but certainly represent sacrifice by the ascending manager and his or her family in some instances.

One of the many challenges that, at the time, annoyed me to no end was Mike's follow-up system. Obviously, some of the action items outlined for execution were less of a priority to me than to Mike. Dragging my feet on working on the item NEVER worked. At some point in the future, sometimes after I had forgotten the item, he would bring the task up, check-mark his notebook for future follow up, and repeat. Needless to say, his persistence paid off in getting things done. I understood the value in this process as my span of influence increased over the years. Regretfully, I improved over time but never reached the precision of his system. Developing proficiency in this area by understanding the method outlined in this book, or your own system, substantially improves managerial results.

Make it easy. Mike taught me early on that if you want something done correctly make it easy for the employees to do. The book outlines that, as a manager, it is your responsibility to provide your team with the resources, tools, time, and methodology to accomplish the task or project. Removing obstacles improves team performance.

In all my interactions with Mike, I found him to be fair and consistent. He focused on improving performance of the people under his direction. Discipline centered on the problem and was delivered without emotion or personal attack. As such, it was generally effective at correcting the issue. Terminating the individual was the last resort; not the objective of the process.

I enjoyed reading Digging Deeper immensely. The book brought back memories of management lessons I learned during my career growth. It also removed a few mysteries in the way Mike dealt with a few issues over the years. If you want to improve your management skills, advance your career, or simply better understand the management perspective, I highly recommend this book. Select the techniques that fit your style for inclusion in your toolbox.

They worked for me, and, based on conversations with other successful individuals, they experienced similar things throughout their careers.

Thank you, Mike, for making this available to aspiring managers.

Wade O. Kemp III

Vice-president and General Manager Ret.
Independent Director
Understudy of Michael Young

DIGGING
DEEPER

Respect your work area, respect your job and company, and treat everyone—whether they work for you, or you for them—respectfully.

SECTION I

SURVEYING

Aerial view of a mine, British Columbia, Canada.

INTRODUCTION

I spent over 35 years actively involved in mining/manufacturing operations, finally leaving management as Vice President of Operations of a midsized mining company. Since then I have consulted in both mining and manufacturing, concentrating on property and process evaluations, due diligence, and tailings retention systems.

This book is a compilation of notes taken over a period of fifty-plus years. These notes cover management, managers, how you as a manager can impact the function of your operation, and how your actions impact your development. I include techniques I've used routinely and those practiced by other successful managers I've observed. There are many very good programs available covering almost all aspects of management. This is not intended to be a complete management manual. It is intended to focus in on the areas where even the best trained managers can stumble and how they can improve.

Throughout this book, I use the words "supervisor," "boss," and "manager" synonymously. I also use the words describing the non-management "subordinate," "employee," "operator," and "worker" synonymously. All of these words are becoming politically incorrect, but I feel that they reflect real life in the corporate world. Teams, to be effective, must have structure where there is a boss and subordinates. How to make the best of this structure is the main purpose of this book.

Why I Wrote This Book

When I was in my mid-thirties, I was made the General Manager of a very big mine, and I was the youngest general manager at any mine in that corporation. I had a transferee in the Health and Safety department who was about my age, and at the end of our first staff meeting together, he asked what my management philosophy was. Well, I realized at that time that in a sense there's no such thing as a philosophy of management, so that's when I started to write down my observations about the decisions I made and why I made them; were they solid, were they not. It forced me, when I wrote something down, to ask myself:

"Does this really make sense in the big picture of management?"

What I want to say in this book is that I have had so much exposure to people and life for the seventy-plus years I've been alive, and had the luck (if you want to call it that) to write down a lot about this experience. I want people to realize that many, if not most, of their experiences in life and work are not unique. Hopefully, this book will show ways these experiences can be handled in a successful manner.

CHAPTER ONE

MANAGEMENT STRUCTURE

Management structures are basically triangles with the larger workforce at the base and the single manager at the top. At the base, an organization is lucky to find one in ten employees with the skills and/or willingness to pay the prices commensurate with promotion. However, as one approaches the top of the triangle a much larger portion of the population is, or thinks they are, ready for the next promotional step. One style of management, therefore, does not work at all levels. You must learn to adjust how you manage as you move up the organization. For example, laying out the workday for your team at the base level is totally necessary, but totally unnecessary, and even destructive, at the top levels of an organization.

Over-supervising at the upper levels:
- Is not cost effective
- Creates the feeling you are not confident in the employees' abilities
- Questions employees' effectiveness
- Questions employees' value or purpose

Under-supervising at the lower levels results in:
- Wasted time while employees wait for direction
- Incorrect work being done
- Priorities missed
- Lost money

The Management Triangle

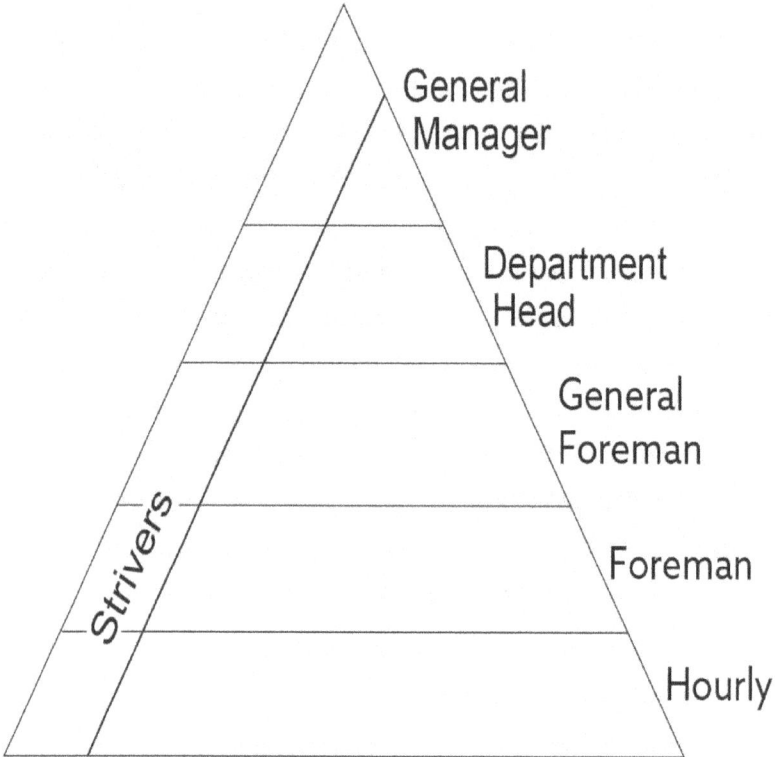

General Manager

Department Head

General Foreman

Foreman

Hourly

Strivers

At each higher level, a larger portion of the people at that level have high expectations for promotion (the "strivers"). The lower you go on the triangle, the larger the overall population and the lower percentage of people with high expectations. At the bottom of the triangle, you manage with many rules, little autonomy, and careful boundaries. At the top of the triangle, the reverse applies. One management style will not fit both the top and the bottom of the Management Triangle.

When speaking of managers, I am referring to the span of first-line supervisors, to general supervisors, to general managers, to vice presidents, to the CEO. I don't differentiate between these levels of management. The first-line supervisor has several people working directly for him or her, and the CEO has several people working directly for him or her; I use the words interchangeably. The technique the CEO uses with subordinates is going to be different, but he or she is still their manager, and advice in the generic sense for first-line supervisors is not that much different than it is for a CEO. The technique might be different, but the way of dealing with people and issues is the same. The second-line supervisor is perhaps the most important individual to the function of an operation. The first-line supervisor deals with the workers directly and in most cases relates more to them than to management. The second-line supervisor will frequently relate to the workers because of his or her background but must relate directly with management and fulfill management needs first. The majority have been promoted to that position because they functioned well as first-line supervisors. However, the majority are not promotable to the next level because of lack of desire, mobility, or education. This majority frequently becomes "infocludes," supervisors who do not allow information to easily flow through them. I cover this in more detail in the Communications section.

CHAPTER TWO

COLLABORATIVE MANAGEMENT

I believe that management needs to be structured. A company <u>cannot</u> be run by consensus.

There are two extremes in management structure:

- Autocratic: Absolute authority. Just one person making all of the decisions.
- Consensus: Majority opinion. Bring a team together, and all decisions are made essentially by vote of that team.

My definition of collaborative management is slightly towards the autocratic side of center. If you have a dozen or so people working on your management team, there must be an acknowledged leader who absolutely makes the final decision on policy. You also want to set up an environment in which the other team members do not feel the least bit intimidated when presenting ideas for consideration by the rest of the team members. They must acknowledge the fact that ultimately, at the end of that meeting or at the end of that project, the only person who can sign off on it is the team leader not the entire team. Their ideas and opinions have been asked for and considered. All of the options—all the positives and negatives—have been thrown out there. The team leader, who is controlling the meeting, must then go around the room, once a plan has been developed, and ask each of the other team members individually if he or she agrees that there is no better solution than the one proposed.

The leader can then finally make the decision to accept that plan.

Most people like to work in that collaborative environment because the majority of them don't really want to be individually held responsible for their decisions. They are more content to contribute part of the input into the decisions but don't want to make the decisions themselves. It is comforting for them to know that there is a person there who is responsible for the decision, and it is not them. Collaborative management gives the team leader sufficient information, based on the expertise of each of the team members, to make an informed final decision, improving the company overall. But, there always has to be a boss who is accountable for the final decision. Regular, well-defined meetings with teams are very effective, but should be run by the manager/supervisor. It should be clear who is in charge and responsible for the actions, if any, that come out of these meetings. The boss in the meetings must possess a certain sense of humility balanced with clearly being the one in charge, in order to get the inclusion of all those people who are experts at the top of their own departments. There is more to the concept of surrounding yourself with good people—they are in their positions because they are good at what they do. You must surround yourself with people whose opinions you trust based on their specific function. You don't want those people to leave a meeting where they were not committed to the solution. Make sure, before you leave that meeting, everyone agrees that the choice being made is the only choice that *can* be made.

I always had an aptitude for getting people to talk to me, because very often they didn't feel particularly threatened by telling me their version of the truth, and it's their version of the truth that is important for me to know—not my version of the truth. Autocrats only get people's version of the truth that they think the autocrat wants. Because autocrats do not welcome input, no one is flowing (i.g., they're afraid to flow) information to the autocrat, so they never know of an opportunity missed. Often, the autocrat is good enough overall that the business survives, but usually doesn't excel. Mine is always the charge to make the business excel; make it the very best it can be. Total autocrats don't get that, they get their individual bests, not necessarily what is best for their companies to excel.

Thinking Outside the Box Carefully

The current push toward consensus management and employees thinking outside the box in many manufacturing and service environments is ineffective and can be counter-productive. In order to achieve the productivity and quality mandated by today's consumer, each and every piece of the supplier's process (manufactured product or service provided) must be analyzed by qualified staff. The correct method(s) must be determined, documented, and disseminated to the workforce. Proper steps need to be taken to make changes. The first step is most important: study and analyze if the change is necessary, and what are the intended and unintended consequences of the change.

Collaborative management, to me, is all about team building, and that means setting up an environment that will encourage employees to think and share outside the box, not act on that thinking. The last thing you want is someone on the production line taking the initiative and changing the process in an effort to be more efficient. Without careful review, the change can have negative, or even dangerous, effects.

Company management should have a process in place that has been fine-tuned over time for making changes. However, in a misguided effort to be modern, they often make the mistake of telling the operator to think outside the box. What you actually want is for the operator to think totally inside the box while operating, and confine his thinking outside the box to team meetings. His motivations for acting outside the box might be perfect, but if the execution suffers, it ruins the quality, could hurt somebody, and ultimately costs rather than saves money.

I've seen team builders, often called facilitators, who do not want to step on the toes of team members in order to solve a problem, even though they know how to solve it. For some reason, they won't force their team into doing the right thing. The team doesn't necessarily know what the right thing is; therefore they can't implement the solution. The team leader must then step up to propose and adopt the proper solution.

As much as most modern managers hate to think tomorrow should be a repeat of today, it is absolutely necessary in most manufacturing and service environments. If change is really necessary in order to attain needed results, then changes of process and procedures— regardless of their origin—must be well-thought-out, managed well, and introduced carefully to assure continued quality of the product or service.

CHAPTER THREE

THE DICHOTOMIES OF MANAGEMENT

The Vicious Circle

One of the major dichotomies of management is dealing with success. You work with your team to become more productive, and you are successful, but your sales stay flat for reasons beyond your control. The only way to overcome this deficiency is to reduce the size or hours of your team. Basically you are asking your team for ways to reduce their numbers or hours. The next attempt to improve team efficiency will not be as easy. What is cost-effective is often defined by someone else.

Through team effort and skill development, your maintenance team makes significant inroads into plant availability and efficiency. With that success comes the pressure to reduce the team size because the plant is running more efficiently, and the maintenance team is less busy. From the team perspective, improvements in efficiency have nothing but negative impacts on them. It seems the only answer is to be sure that when the reductions of cost in staff occur, they are taken care of through attrition (employee retirement or normal quit/resignation) or assignment to different functions (for example, maintenance people can be assigned to construction projects). Teams just won't cooperate with efficiency efforts if one of them has to lose his or her job to get there.

In my experience, downsizing is unfortunate—it always has been—but it is unavoidable. Despite belief to the contrary, this is exactly the reason why most companies are reluctant to hire new employees to meet a surge in demand. Instead, they will usually use overtime as long as possible. There is always a cost involved with a layoff, but just as importantly, management doesn't want to go through the traumatic—and it is traumatic—process of a layoff.

Popular jargon these days is that big bad companies are now using layoffs as an unfair method to reduce costs. Layoffs are not even close to being a recent greedy phenomenon. If a business does not have the sales, for whatever reason, sufficient to support its work force, it has no option but to reduce that force—period.

When I first became master mechanic, supervising the maintenance team at a mine where I worked, I was getting called out after hours to the plant five times per week to deal with maintenance issues. When I left that position three years later, I was going out for that purpose once a month or so. I certainly look at that as a success; that we changed the operation from a breakdown maintenance to a preventive one. Unfortunately, that meant the team was not as busy and the first thing that happened as a result of our success was pressure from upper management to reduce the maintenance team. I was able to minimize the negative impact on the team by assigning members to project work that had customarily been contracted out, then allowed attrition to reduce the force if still needed.

Determining Wages

One of the criteria for determining supervisory wages in most companies is the number of teams or team members supervised. The bigger the number, the bigger the pay. A manager realizes he could significantly reduce operating costs by combining two departments. He also realizes that he will have fewer direct reports thus exposing himself to demotion. So, even at the higher ranks in a corporation, there is a negative incentive to reduce people. An incentive to increase efficiency must be infused at all levels of an organization.

The Wage Gap

If a person has a skill set that makes money, then they (can) make money. The person with the skill set to drive a truck, for example, but not the skill set to be a stock broker, will be able to earn truck driver wages not stock trader money. Listening to people crying about others that have the skill set to make money—a skill set they don't have—is very frustrating to me.

Often I hear that despite people getting a better education, their salaries are not keeping up with others. However, what I never hear is the other side of that statement, which is what kind of education they are getting. Are these degrees that historically make money, or are they degrees in skill sets that historically don't make money?

If it's the latter, that's the explanation for it. Education, in itself, does not assure monetary success. The education you receive often reflects your skill set, and that combination of skill set, education, and willingness to pay the price of career success, dictates your future earnings capability.

Manager Training and Promotion

Corporations often send their managers to management training classes. Usually the motive is to get them to be better managers, thus expecting them to implement the changes they've learned at training. Because introspection and accepting fault is so difficult, the individuals usually return with nothing gained. Each manager embodies some of the qualifications of a manager, so during the training, individual managers find reinforcement for their strengths, and downplay the effect or don't recognize the training that keys in on their weaknesses. Management training lacks "train the trainer" education aspects. The people at the top of the organization must fully embrace the tenants of the training. The lower levels of management will react to and emulate upper management style, long before they will react to a training style that is contrary to the reality of their company/business.

When subordinates are being considered for promotion, their weaknesses (as well as their strengths) are usually identified. Despite knowing these weaknesses, and before promoting the subordinate, many managers, after the "honeymoon period," begin to evaluate that subordinate on those weaknesses, not the strengths. Trying to change a weakness is going to run a manager headfirst into the problem of personality changes. If you know the weakness beforehand, work on strengthening it; don't make it the only judgment criteria.

Give focus and direction to the employee:
- Set expectations on promotion
- State weaknesses
- Set expectations to improve

- Allow the opportunity to improve
- Evaluate

Safety

Often, corporations wonder why groups within the organization will live with potentially unsafe equipment or practices. The truth is that all managers work within a budget and are primarily evaluated on their ability to meet demand while staying within their budget. If a costly potential safety item comes up during the budget cycle, then it usually won't get done because it's not in the budget. The only solution is to have the company, instead of the individual manager, take responsibility for the cost of the fix and incentivizing the finding of these issues or practices.

Elliot Lake Miners Memorial.

CHAPTER FOUR

PAYING THE PRICE
TO BE IN MANAGEMENT

Upward Mobility

The upwardly mobile person is someone who wants to do what is necessary to move to the top of an organization.

The upwardly mobile person can't base basic career decisions on factors such as family and where to live and still expect to receive all of the benefits of an upwardly mobile career.

If you want to stay rooted in your local community, but the corporate headquarters are not locally based, you can't expect to be part of upper management. If you want to be in management and part of the corporate world, chances are you are going to have to move to where the opportunities exist and go where the work is. You have to make some very earth-shattering decisions with your life in terms of family and where you want to live in order to move up. You can't expect a job in your field to come to you. I've seen so many people who are management material. They are well-educated, have been performing technical jobs their entire career, and never leave the small town they live in. They like where they live, they really love their community, and they have family there. They are willing to live with whatever comes their way. Some of them get frustrated, but know they have to make a life decision and live with it. Some of them get upset because they are not moving up in the company as they feel they should, but they are not willing to take the steps and make the sacrifices one must make to be upwardly mobile in a career. Your biggest detractor in your upward mobility is yourself, and you can rarely have things both ways.

I was in mining management, which meant I didn't have a lot of choices in where to live much less put down roots. I had to live where the mines were, and mines are usually in very remote areas; in the "middle of nowhere" kind of places. I had to make the decision for myself and my family to live where my profession and livelihood took me. I will note, though, that every time I moved my family to a new location, it was for either a promotion in the company I worked for, or it was a new position that was higher up (bigger salary and more responsibility) than the one I left. I was upwardly mobile. Wherever I was, I made it 'home.'

The Prices one must pay:
- Must move to jobs
- Must spend the time needed to make the operation work—no matter what
- Family time often must take second place
- Carry the burden of worry and frustration
- Must be able to separate personal from professional life
- Your decisions are often final and accountable
- Must learn company politics–you have to work with/for others constructively
- You are only as effective as your ability to get your boss (company) to do what you think is necessary

My goal was to be the youngest general manager of an operation within the corporation. I succeeded in that goal, because I was willing to pay the price associated with that success.

SECTION II

YOU

*When you go into management, if you don't get people to work **for** you, you're not going to be a successful manager.*

Supervising at a lead mine during a visit of corporate executives, Missouri, USA; 1974.

Malcolm Mitchell, a young standout football player from the University of Georgia, talked to his now-famous ladies book club about how he was not nearly as proud of his football playing as he was of his ability to read. Why? His football skill came naturally; he had to work hard to learn how to read.

Consider that from the perspective of being a manager. There are few people that are gifted with most of the skills needed to be a good manager. The rest of us must work on those areas of management skills that don't come naturally in order to be a good manager. Those skills, once achieved will be sources of pride. I am very proud, for instance, that I can control my temper now, something I couldn't do early in my career.

Most of the notes throughout this book are about YOU, and how YOU, as a supervisor, can set an effective career path by developing a basic set of accepted management skills. The decisions you make define YOU. You have to dictate your career yourself through the decisions you make each and every day. You have to make the tough decisions that most people back away from. You have command of your future with the decisions YOU make.

It is important to note there is no such thing as a perfect manager. To be perfect, the manager would have to be in perfect sync with you and that cannot happen. Even the good ones have flaws that you, as a subordinate, live with. Only when these flaws become too numerous or too basic will that manager move from being a good one to being a bad one in your eyes.

I have never worked for a perfect manager, nor have I ever considered myself a perfect manager, but I'd like to think that I would fit the 'good' category. I've worked with a few good managers and a larger number of bad ones. The bottom line is that the odds are very much in favor of your having to work for bad managers most of your career. It is important, therefore, for you to develop a personal style that will rank you at least in the good category, and you will learn how to deal with bad bosses.

CHAPTER FIVE

YOUR PERFORMANCE AS MANAGER

Consistency is key to your performance. People around you will perform much better if you show up each day with the same attitude about them and the job. Bosses with bad attitudes don't get good performance out of their team, but believe it or not, a boss with a consistent bad attitude will get more from the team than one that is attitudinally up and down.

How to Know if Someone is a Good Facilities Manager

I am most familiar with the mining industry, and one of the ways to instantly know if you have a good manager at a mine is to go out for a ride into their mine. If it's a smooth ride, you probably have a good manager, and if it's a bumpy ride, you probably have a bad manager. Anyone who runs heavy equipment and doesn't recognize that a perfectly smooth road is vital, is not a good manager.

Some people are neat and some are sloppy. Sloppy has no place in the work environment. Sloppy creates tripping and other hazards; but just as importantly it creates the wrong attitude about the work environment. Many peoples' home environment would not meet company standards, so each day they have to adjust to an unfamiliar environment. Government and corporate inspectors get, and usually keep, a negative first impression of a sloppy work place. The corporate bosses get the negative or positive feedback about the manager, and that affects the manager's job. The government inspectors get an impression of a plant in terms of safety and preventing accidents. This affects the corporation negatively in terms of the cost in fines (which will also affect the manager's job in the eyes of the corporate bosses).

MSHA is the mining equivalent of OSHA. MSHA stands for Mining Safety and Health Administration (OSHA is Occupational Safety and Health Administration).

One significant difference between the two agencies is that OSHA sends inspectors to the job site after an accident occurs. MSHA sends inspectors to the mines at least quarterly to make sure facilities are run in a manner to avoid accidents.

A government inspector will walk into a facility and instantly form an opinion about how well a plant is run. If the plant has nice clean roads, flower boxes actually have flowers growing in them, the tinwork is actually tinwork, not rust work; the inspector will get the impression that this is a well-run operation.

During the inspection, if the agent sees nothing but clean facilities and compliance with the safety rules—all conveyor walkways are free of hazards, for example—and he walks up a conveyor and sees a flag for an emergency shutdown is off, he may just say, "Maybe you should just take care of that." He doesn't pull out his ticket book (as soon as he pulls out his ticket book it's on your record permanently, and you'll be fined), and he'll give you a break based on his overall impression of your plant. It is a well-run operation. He's not after a well-run operation, he's after a poorly run operation. If that inspector comes into your plant and it's trashy looking, and he's tripping all over the place trying to get up that same conveyer, and he sees that emergency switch that is slightly off, he will write you a ticket right then and there.

Self-Evaluation

Be very careful that you are measuring your own performance using the same criteria that your boss uses in his evaluation of you. Most first-line supervisors achieved their position because of their skills and experience in the work place. Once they get into supervision, they will often continue to judge themselves on their ability to use their particular skill set while their supervisor is judging them on their supervisory and planning skills. Most times, these evaluations are very different. A supervisor that constantly works with his team (getting dirty) but frequently misses paperwork deadlines is going to be surprised with poor performance ratings. Putting in long hours and effectively doing your subordinate's job does not make you a good supervisor.

Anticipation

Think two to three steps down the road,
you find yourself not tripping as often…

A key part of being able to manage companies is anticipating: what you do today is going to impact tomorrow. You need to use your experiences to have the foresight to look two or three steps ahead in production and know what's going to happen next. You then need to analyze how the company's current actions could have a negative impact on processes. This is not natural to a lot of people, but I think it's natural to the people who do well in corporations. Thinking ahead and realizing that doing something will affect production, and in turn visualizing how it will affect customers and their production, is a critical thinking skill that successful supervisors must have and continue to develop.

Upper management can be extremely myopic from the standpoint that the only justification for process improvement is an increase in capacity. However, more capacity usually requires more sales first. So the process is not improved or updated, making it more difficult to compete in a tight market. When you do get the chance for process improvement, before that process improvement happens, you need to look upstream and downstream to identify consequences, both intended and unintended. Increasing efficiency in one area often will lead to a bottleneck in another point of the production line. Each of these bottlenecks, if addressed, will cumulatively increase overall capacity. The result will be to improve the overhead costs immediately by reducing hours worked to produce standard volumes, and you're going to have capacity that you can sell in the future.

Contingency Planning

Always give hourly crew assignments with the assumption that everything will go according to plan. Then give a back-up assignment if/when something goes wrong. Many, if not most, employees will wait for direction when a job goes wrong. Supervisors, despite their wish for creative team thinking, get upset if an employee tries to solve a problem on his own (and screws up) or leaves the work site to seek help and the supervisor has to hunt him down. If you find a team standing around waiting for a solution to a problem that has them stopped, it's the supervisor's fault for not having assigned a back-up job, not having established a management contact method, or not having provided the skills or tools needed to complete the job. The supervisor is responsible whether it goes right or wrong.

You must understand all the aspects of your responsibilities. When you are caught unprepared for a surge in demand, or any unexpected crisis to your process or service, you cannot comfort yourself in not knowing there was a plan for the surge that you were not privy to. If plans are not volunteered to you by your management, then you must ask for them as many times as it takes to get them. If the plans don't exist, and surges happen, then the good manager will devise, with the team, cost effective ways to deal with surges.

Managing Your Managers

As you move up in management, you don't manage every day, but a good manager always has a way of checking the pulse of the team and their actions. For example, you have a department head who is responsible for maintenance of equipment. You have a way of measuring how the department is being managed without really being overt about it. There are indicators that you can watch for, and then see if things may be moving in the wrong direction such as daily sheets, reports, or something you may have seen as you walked through the plant. That's where I would ask questions all the time. I would go out to different parts of the plant and ask certain questions—non-threatening questions—and I would know what was going on in a specific department just by asking. The maintenance superintendent is responsible for the maintenance costs, and if costs start to move out of whack, that superintendent is letting his costs get out of control. The two of you need to sit down and carefully walk through what is going on in that department, and work it out. Talk to that supervisor about it; don't wait until he gets into trouble. He doesn't feel like he is being micromanaged, and you're still paying attention to the bottom line.

Staying Organized

With so many variables going on in a manager's day-to-day duties, you have to find a way to stay organized. If you have photographic memory, then great for you, but for the other 99% of us that do not, one *has* to figure out a way to stay organized. Unless you develop your own way to keep all of those things in order, you are going to miss things; and you will not be able to effectively do your job. Of course, everyone is different in learning and retaining information. So, it is up to you to develop your own systems, and organize yourself in a way that works best for you.

The way I stay best organized is to actually write things down. I know and understand that a weakness I have is that I don't have a photographic memory, so I know the only way for me to remember things accurately is to write them down. I don't use a smart phone or computer for this; that doesn't work for me. I prepare for meetings by writing my lists of questions and agenda items I need to cover, and I take notes in those meetings. As I evaluate the people who work for me, I make notes of my observations of them, so when it is time to make their formal evaluation, I can refer to my notes so I can give them the best, most complete and accurate evaluation.

I make organizational charts, color coded with the information I need and space for the shorthand note of the pertinent points for the conversation with each person or meeting agenda.

FOLLOWUP LOG	J	K	M	J	M	FURTHER NOTES AND FOLLOW-UP
ISSUE	L	W	M	D	Y	
CM - taxes/LLC, recording					11/5	
Copy WOK, KW reports						
Copy of report			11/5			JD copied 10/13
WOK re politics, future etc					11/5	TK to MA, KJ future short, WOK to ?
HYT info request						
Mfg meeting re: project X	11/9					JB alone, long discussion before
Items in 2016						

An example of my meeting/phone call notes. I have devised codes and shorthand notes that work best for me and the way I work: questions or agenda I need to express to a specific person. There are many tasks; this is my way of keeping on top of everything that I need to accomplish, and make certain nothing is missed. I can always refer back to this chart to make sure I covered a certain subject if it comes up at a later date, and I can't recall the necessary details off the top of my head. I can then look up the email or paperwork referred to in my chart.

You don't have to know or remember all of the information, you just need to know where to find it.

Multitasking

I believe the word "multitasking" is too cliché-ish. To me, multitasking means you have to take care of everything that is on your plate. Nowadays, some call it multitasking; I call it the job. When you start out in supervision at the first-line level, you are just responsible for taking care of eight or ten people and just basically one function, but you're starting to learn how to deal with people, to deal with your boss, to deal with meeting orders, etc. When you came up from the ranks, this may have been foreign to you. Your first step into supervision comes with multiple tasks to juggle compared to your entry-level position. When a degreed employee, such as an engineer who does technical drawings, transfers into a supervisory role, all of a sudden he is supervising multiple people doing multiple tasks, and he is doing more than what he did as a supervised employee. Bottom line, you're dealing with a results orientation, and have to be organized and work on many different things at the same time. The word "multitasking" is the job description of a manager.

I worked for a period of time in the Midwestern part of the United States. The mines were set right square in the middle of farm and timber country. The guys who came to work in the underground mines; that was only half their day. The other half was when they went home at the end of their shift and did their logging, worked in their car repair garage, or worked on their farm. I would see guys that went underground for the day shift, walk right straight through the clean room and not stop to change out of their dirty clothes or shower, but just walk right out the doors to go to their next job. These were hardworking people, and their farms—or whatever their family business happened to be—were the most important thing to them. They were not going to give that up to go to the mines, even though it was more money. They just pulled two jobs at once. That may be, to some people, the definition of multitasking. I say that was just how life was for those people.

CHAPTER SIX

PERCEPTION

The most important thing about YOU is that as a manager, how you perceive *yourself* is quite irrelevant. As a manager you are getting your job done through others, so the most important perception of you is that of those around you. You must listen to the people around you and watch their reaction to you if you really want to find out how they perceive you. Asking them will seldom give you a clear answer since there are too many risks for them to tell the truth—especially if you are not a particularly good supervisor. Being human, we will downplay the importance of the skills and traits we lack, and play up those that we have; those we supervise will do the exact opposite. A manager who can instinctively solve mechanical problems but has poor personal hygiene will inevitably be considered a poor boss because of his (to him) minor weakness of smelling bad.

At a large mine where I worked, they had a program where they would bring in a group of peers, subordinates, and supervisors, who worked at that mine, once every other year. They had a list of about 50 holistic questions they used to evaluate the managers in the company. Each person in the group had 5 or 6 names on his or her questionnaire. So, they had to quickly answer each question for each person, thus giving an instinctive versus a thought-out answer. They would take the results that were computer-generated and give you just the summarization of what people thought of you. I got my first one when I was the engineer/general foreman, and I came up with an average score. I was able to read all the areas in which I was sub-substandard (by my standards), and I found that to be unacceptable. I set a goal to change, correct my faults, and get a better score the next time the evaluation took place. Two years later the evaluation was run again, and that time I received a rating of 'outstanding' because I was able to change those things to the point that I actually got promoted into a much bigger job. Everything I was faulted on, I made a point to correct. It worked, and I was made the youngest general manager in the history of that mining company. It was my goal to be the youngest GM at that mine, and I succeeded because I made a point to find out what others thought my faults were, and I changed. It was not easy. Achieving goals rarely is. I really had to work at changing, but I did, and I was rewarded for my efforts.

The following two pages are excerpted from the "Talent Inventory Feedback Appraisal" given by the company I worked for. The criteria were broken down into "Management Practices" sections, and the six "Appraisers." Although each time the individuals were different it always consisted of at least one from a management level above me, at least two at a similar level, and the rest from a lower level. Each Appraiser would be familiar with me, and worked with me in the prior two years. These appraisers scored my performance based on their perceptions of, and interactions with, me and my management and decision-making.

METAL MINING DIVISION

T A L E N T   I N V E N T O R Y   F E E D B A C K
APPRAISALS DATED 1977

MICHAEL C YOUNG   GEN MGR STAFF

MANAGEMENT PRACTICES

R S O A   COMMUNICATING

3 3   *WHEN HE COMMUNICATES TO OTHERS, HE COULD BE EXPECTED TO BE
             VAGUE AND AMBIGUOUS.
        6   WHEN CONFRONTED WITH INPLEMENTING A SUPERVISORY DECISION
             WHICH HE STONGLY BELIEVES IS WRONG, HE COULD BE EXPECTED TO
             SPEAK UP AND TELL HIS SUPERVISOR WHY HE BELIEVES IT IS WRONG.

                              WORK RELATIONS

    1 1 4   WHEN ANOTHER INDIVIDUAL MAKES A MISTAKE, HE COULD BE EXPECTED
             TO AVOID BROADCASTING THE FACT, AND INSTEAD CONTACT THE
             INDIVIDUAL DIRECTLY TO RESOLVE THE PROBLEM.
    2 3 1   *WHEN PRESENTED WITH A NEW APPROACH, HE COULD BE EXPECTED TO
             SAY "IT WON'T WORK" AND MAKE EXCUSES FOR NOT TRYING IT.

                                SUPERVISING

      3 3   WHEN SETTING GOALS WITH SUBORDINATES, HE COULD BE EXPECTED TO
             FOLLOW-UP AND REVIEW THEIR PERFORMANCE AGAINST GOALS.
    2 1 3   WHEN SETTING GOALS WITH SUBORDINATES, HE COULD BE EXPECTED TO
             SET DIFFICULT BUT ATTAINABLE GOALS THAT STRETCH HIS SUBORDINATES
      2 4   WHEN A SUBORDINATE PERFORMS UNSATISFACTORILY, HE COULD BE
             EXPECTED TO TELL HIM WHAT IS EXPECTED AND FORLLOW-UP LATER WITH
             FREQUENT REVIEWS OF PERFOEMANCE.
      1 5   HE COULD BE EXPECTED TO COMMUNICATE WITH HIS SUBORDINATES
             TO GET INFORMATION ON WORK ACCOMPLISHMENTS AND WORK PROBLEMS
             AND TO ENCOURAGE ACTION TO OVERCOME JPROBLEMS.
      2 4   HE COULD BE EXPECTED TO DEVELOP HIS SUBORDINATES FOR FUTURE
             ORGANIZATIONAL REQUIREMENTS.

                           PLANNING & ORGANIZING

      2 4   HE COULD BE EXPECTED TO DEMONSTRATE FORESIGHT AND TAKE ACTION
             TO ACHIEVE LONG RANGE GOALS RATHER THAN SIMPLY CONCENTRATE ON
             DAY-TO-DAY TASKS.
      3 3   WHEN CALLED UPON FOR INFORMATION, ANALYSIS, AND ANSWERS, HE
             COULD BE EXPECTED TO PROVIDE AND ACCURATE, THOROUGH, AND COMPLETE
             PIECE OF WORK.
        6   HE COULD BE EXPECTED TO DEVELOP SHORT AND LONG RANGE PLANS TO
             IMPROVE PRODUCTIVITY.
      5 1   INSTEAD OF WAITING FOR PROBLEMS TO ARISE, HE COULD BE EXPECTED
             TO ANTICIPATE POTENTIAL PROBLEMS AND SOLVE THEM BEFORE THEY
             DEVELOP INTO A PROBLEM.

    R = RARELY, S = SOMETIMES O = OFTEN A = ALMOST ALWAYS
    * INNEFECTIVE PRACTICE

METAL MINING DIVISION

T A L E N T   I N V E N T O R Y   F E E D B A C K
APPRAISALS DATED 1977

MICHAEL C YOUNG   GEN MGR STAFF

PERFORMANCE AGREEMENTS

FINAL CLASSIFICATION   EXCEPTIONAL PERFORMER   EXCEPTIONAL PERFORMER   3
                                                 TOP PERFOEMER   3
AVERAGE CLASSIFICATION   EXCEPTIONAL PERFORMER   EFFECTIVE PERFORMER   0
                                                 SATISFACTORY PERFORMER   0
NUMBER OF APPRAISERS   SIX (6)   NOT CURRENTLY CLASSIFIED 0

MANAGEMENT PRACTICES

R S O A

PROBLEM SOLVING / DECISION MAKING

4 2   WHEN REQUESTED TO GATHER INFORMATION ABOUT A WORK PROBLEM,
      HE COULD BE EXPECTED TO INVESTIGATE THOROUGHLY AND RELIABLY
      ALL THE FACTS RELATING TO THE PROBLEM.
6   *WHEN CONFRONTED WITH A PROBLEM, HE COULD BE EXPECTED TO HAVE
        DIFFICULTY MAKING A DECISION.
  1 5   WHEN A CRITICAL PROBLEM ARISES WHICH REQUIRES A TEAM EFFORT,
        HE COULD BE EXPECTED TO COORDINATE EFFECTIVELY SUCH AN EFFORT
        AND GET THE PROBLEM SOLVED QUICKLY.
3 3   *IF FACED WITH A DIFFICULT, UNPOPULAR DECISION, HE COULD BE
        EXPECTED TO DENY A PROBLEM EXISTS AND FAIL TO MAKE THE
        UNPOPULAR DECISION.
  1 2 3 WHEN WORKING ON MANY DIFFERENT ASSIGNMENTS AT THE SAME TIME,
        HE COULD BE EXPECTED TO WEIGH ALL THE FACTS AND DECIDE ON
        THE BEST ORDER OF PRIORITY.
    3 3 WHEN FACED WITH A CRITICAL PERSONNEL PROBLEM, HE COULD BE
        EXPECTED TO MEET THE PROBLEM HEAD ON AND TAKE TIMELY, DIRECT
        AND INTELLIGENT ACTION TO RESOLVE THE PROBLEM.

DIERCT ACTION

3 3   *WHEN REQUESTED TO HANDLE AN IMPORTANT AND URGENT TASK, HE
        COULD BE EXPECTED TO TAKE LONGER THAN NECESSARY TO COMPLETE
        THE TASK.
    6   HE COULD BE EXPECTED TO FAMILIARIZE HIMSELF THOROUGHLY WITH
        CURRENT TECHNICAL KNOWLEDGE IN HIS AREA OF RESPONSIBILITY.
  5 1   WHEN HE MAKES A COMMITMENT, HE COULD BE EXPECTED TO MEET THAT
        COMMITMENT.
    6   WHEN FACED WITH NUMEROUS OBSTACLES AND OTHERS SAYING "IT CAN'T
        BE DONE", HE COULD BE EXPECTED TO TAKE A POSITIVE APPROACH
        AND SUCCESSFULLY COMPLETE THE TASK.
  2 4   WHEN GIVEN GENERAL INSTRUCTIONS, HE COULD BE EXPECTED TO HANDLE
        THE MATTER WITH VERY LITTLE CUIDANCE AND DIRECTION.
4 2   *WHEN SUGGESTIONS ARE MADE FOR CORRECTION POOR WORK BEHAVBIOR,
        HE COULD BE EXPECTED TO TAKE A "LET'S NOT ROCK THE BOAT"
        POSTITION.

R = RARELY S = SOMETIMES O = OFTEN A = ALMOST ALWAYS
* INNEFECTIVE PRACTICE

Lacking a formal program that defines how others perceive you, it is possible to do it on your own. Watch how people react to you. A team that does not like looking you in the face, or is never smiling, or is evasive in their replies to your questions *does not* think you are a good supervisor. Again, your ability to function in supervision is largely the way others perceive you versus how you perceive yourself.

You can change if you recognize:
1. What you are lacking.
2. You <u>want</u> to change it.

During your performance appraisal, your boss (or a coworker) may indicate a trait of yours that hinders your effectiveness. Since it had to be brought to your attention, you didn't recognize it as a problem. For example, in meetings, you have a habit of answering questions directed at a peer because you are quicker to recall the answer (or you want everyone to know how smart you are). This habit often makes the peer feel angry or unimportant. You should carefully determine if you want to eliminate that trait. If you decide not to change that behavior (in other words you don't think of it as negative trait), then don't change it. But you will be responsible for that choice and the possible career consequences. If you do want to change, have the boss pick a signal that only you recognize, and have the boss indicate to you each time it is observed while you're doing it.

I had an engineer working for me who was super qualified for his job and had a desire to be promoted. His downfall though, was that when asked a basic question, he would go back to the very origin of his answer and take forever to get to the point. So, I told him that taking too long to answer a question was a key problem in dealing with people, and that causes people to get very frustrated. We ended up working out a plan between us to keep him in check. Early in our working relationship, he had complimented me by saying I had qualities conducive to 'Zen' thinking. If we were sitting in a meeting and he started to go on too long with his points, I would just quietly say 'Zen' right in the middle of his conversation, so he would know that he was doing it; and it worked very well. He learned to back off of those unnecessary details quite dramatically.

CHAPTER SEVEN

SINGING THE COMPANY SONG

It seems that the popular attitude today is to revile corporate America. Therefore, in many employees' eyes, it seems appropriate to have no loyalty to the company they work for. One of the reasons for this disloyalty is the seeming endless news of corporate greed, overpaid executives, and environmental catastrophes. No doubt some companies and individuals exist that deserve this condemnation; however many, if not most, do not.

Attitude Is Infectious

If you decide to become a supervisor/manager you must learn to "sing the company song." You are the representative of the company to those you supervise. If you present a negative attitude toward the company, the people you supervise will develop the same attitude. Quality, safety, and efficiency will all suffer as a result.

Harsh as it may seem, if you can't "sing the company song" and haven't tried to work with your supervisors to solve the issues causing the negative attitude—you must leave the company. You are doing yourself, your subordinates (the team you are managing), and the company, no good.

When most companies recruit, a key personality trait they look for is enthusiasm. A brilliant recruit with a "ho hum" attitude is not as valuable as a recruit with just average skills, but has a fire in his belly. A company with a team that really wants the company to succeed will more than likely succeed.

Mood Is Contagious

If you present a constant can-do attitude, your team will have a good chance of picking up the same attitude. A grouchy, unhappy supervisor begets a similar team—one that does not respond well to tough conditions. If you're not happy with your job, how can your team be happy?

I can vividly remember my transformation each morning upon arriving at work. While driving to work I would be thinking about all the tough things/decisions of the day ahead and be in, at best, a contemplative mood. However, by the time I opened the office door I was cheerful and upbeat. Over time, this demeanor became natural at work, allowing me to be upbeat virtually all the time without working at it.

It is usually quite easy to see how a team is managed just by looking at the team members' faces and demeanor. Watch how a team functions as a group. Open faces and a willingness to help and exchange ideas indicate an open management style, while downcast, unresponsive faces tend to indicate an autocratic, vindictive style.

Temper Is Communicable

You cannot lose your temper and be a good supervisor. Many supervisors that do yell and lose their temper easily, excuse it in their mind. They self-justify by thinking the occasion warranted that degree of response and that they were under control. However, that is not how the *recipient* perceives the action. A temper is definitely something each of us can learn to control. It's easier to control a temper than to deal with the aftermath. Over the past several decades we have all found that we can stop using politically incorrect actions and verbiages just by consciously stopping them. The same is true with a temper. First you have to decide you don't want it in the work place, then work on stopping it each time it rears itself. Eventually calm reactions will become a habit. In other words, make an intentional effort to stop the temper even if it feels fake. Soon it will become natural.

I lost two promotions early in my career because of my temper. I would say the last ten years of my professional career, most people didn't even recognize I had a temper, and that was all a result of control. I had to make a conscious effort, and it was very difficult for me, especially at the start of my transformation. In my last position, where I managed several mines with hundreds of people and a plethora of problems, I had a whole bunch of things annoying me; and yet, through it all, no one ever saw my temper. Annoyed, yes; temper, no.

I had one boss in a lead mining business whose temper and volume of his anger were so bad, we had to line his office with lead sheet to keep the noise down. In part because I learned to control my temper and remain upbeat, that boss—the very one who originally held back promotions due to my temper—became my most important mentor, and the person responsible for much of my future successes with that company. Through it all, his office needed the lead lining until he was promoted to a far-away corporate office.

There Are No Jobs in Your Organization That Are Beneath You

Ex*ample:* One day you're walking into the office and there is a dangerous patch of ice on the parking lot. You work in the office and have no responsibility in that area. If you are a good manager, you will not make the observation that "someone should fix that." Instead, just make sure it does get fixed. Go directly to the responsible party, put salt on it yourself, mark it—do something, but don't just say that "someone should fix that."

The same applies to non-safety issues. A costly bad operating practice should receive a similar amount of corrective effort. There are no jobs in your organization that are beneath you. If you're the big boss and are normally the first to get to work each morning, empty the lunch room dish washer when you get your coffee instead of expecting one of the clerks to do it. That will be noticed and appreciated.

Don't be guilty of looking for problems in other areas to deflect attention from problems in your own area. However, if you see costly problems outside your area of responsibility make a concerted effort to get to the people who are responsible. Share your observations and if possible your ideas on how to solve the problem. An underlying theme to these notes is to try to provide answers, not just questions and/or complaints.

A good idea to improve safety, environment, or cost cannot be brought up just once. Don't expect it to fix itself without work or effort. Many times, when a good idea is identified, someone in the organization will say, "Well, I told them that should be fixed a long time ago." A good employee, especially a supervisor, should feel a *responsibility* to find a way to get that good idea reviewed by the people that can make it a reality in a timely manner. Saying (or thinking) it once is only a part of your responsibility. Procuring action is the most important part.

If you find you are just putting in eight hours per day to get a paycheck, you cannot be a good supervisor. If you are not getting promotions you think you deserve, this could be one big reason. A bored supervisor is easy to spot and quite un-promotable. Find jobs or tasks that get you cranked up because enthusiasm is infectious and leads to promotion.

Never Ever Treat Someone as if They Are Dumb

The janitor, usually one of the lowest paid positions in an organization, probably thinks he or she is just as smart as the CEO but just hasn't had the opportunities needed to get there. Seldom will employees think they are in that lowly position because they are dumb and will resent being treated as if they are. Some of the most intelligent people I have encountered are under-educated and doing menial work for a living. Never forget, the plant/office will notice the janitor is missing long before they will miss the manager.

Create Situations Where People Know
Their Value to the Organization

Very often supervisors can be heard saying, *"I wonder why they don't understand?"* when referring to non-management team members. This can happen when the company is in union negotiations and tough decisions need to be made.

It is necessary to recognize that not everyone is wired the same. The worst question management can ask about their employees is why they don't understand something from the manager's perspective.

The reason is quite simple: you are in management because you thrive on leadership and solving problems. As a manager, you don't think like the operator. Most hourly employees thrive on being very skilled in one position or discipline. The average supervisor makes a lousy truck driver and the average truck driver makes a lousy supervisor. Both are totally necessary, but require totally different mind-sets. That is why "they don't understand," and "they" don't understand why you don't understand. Don't expect non-management to think like management and vice versa. If he thought like you, he would be in management.

My son-in-law's father was a very active member of the IBEW (International Brotherhood of Electrical Workers); a craftsman. Against the odds we became good friends. He worked for several years on the Alaska Pipeline. His view of the pipeline was a long period of secure good paying work, while mine would have been: "This is going to take forever. How can I get it done quicker so I can move on to the next project?"

Same project with two almost opposite, very important, views.

Some people don't want to be in management. As a manager, you may not understand that mind-set, but that doesn't make it wrong. A good truck driver has the unique mind-set that allows him or her to completely focus on doing one thing safely and correctly, hour upon hour. A management mind-set in that work setting would be dangerous and expensive as that mind drifts to other things when focus is mandatory. Those people are satisfied where they are in their job. That is ok! You must try to motivate subordinates by *their* standards, not yours. Supervisors need to create situations where people know their value to the organization.

So many managers put pressure on first-line supervisors to have a plan for moving up in management, and nine out of ten of those guys just want to stay where they are. What they are generally looking for is a steady job that they are going to have when they retire, without a lot of hassle. They don't want to be in there making the big decisions, they just want to do it without thinking too hard about it.

Rank-and-file employees are not focused on what's happening with the economics of the company, so don't expect them to be thinking that way. They don't want to pay the price to be in management. They like where they live, they like what they do, and when they're done doing it, they like to do what they do after their work day is finished. They like putting the day behind and going home to their families, and that is a huge part of their lives. They don't really desire to move up, and they're ok with where they are in the company.

Again, good management will watch for and work with that ten percent who have the skill-set and desire to move into management. Bad management will identify good skilled employees and promote them without determining if they have management skills and desires, often losing them as managers and skilled employees because they can't make the mental transition to management.

If you can find the one truck driver in ten who wants to be a supervisor and help that one through the process, I still have to deal successfully with the other nine who have the mental fix that most managers don't have: they can put their mind in gear and keep it there and keep their trucks safe. They keep a routine, which is something most managers can't do. Eight to ten hours a day of driving into a mine and back out without causing an accident and taking care of the heavy vehicles requires focus, and it takes a certain kind of person to mentally be able to do that. Not everyone can. It's a very important part of the overall operation. Management people can't think like that.

Double Up

Very often you will have to do double duty. You will find yourself working for a boss who does not understand the duties and responsibilities of your job. When the boss instructs you to do ineffective things to solve problems in your area of responsibility, you must react positively to his instructions, but you will then have to double your efforts and also do what needs to get done without countering the boss's instructions. That means you need to implement the boss's ideas. Since that will not resolve the issue, you *also* need to find the root cause of the problem, and solve it the correct way. For example, the boss sees a messy work area and insists on disciplining those involved. You couch your discipline in a <u>constructive</u> manner while setting up and implementing a training program so the production crew can do their jobs correctly and avoid the problem resurfacing; the real solution to the problem. This is a tough duty, but remember, a failure in your area of responsibility is a reflection on you—not the boss.

The old cliché, "lead by example," is extremely important. You cannot expect your team to have a clean working area when your office is a pigsty. You cannot expect your team to enthusiastically work a cold outside job when you are sitting in in your warm office with your feet up on your desk reading a newspaper and drinking a cup of coffee. Work the way you want/expect your team to work. "Do as I say, not as I do" doesn't work anywhere in life.

Admit There Are Things Others Do Better Than You

The majority of NBA coaches are much shorter and less physically talented that the players they coach. The coaches are, however, very effective at getting the most out of the player's talents. The same dynamic happens in the work place. You may have little talent for welding but can still supervise welders by recognizing and directing their skills. Be proud they are part of your team. Pride is not the same thing as taking credit for something; it is more of a team feeling.

CHAPTER EIGHT

THE MANAGER/EMPLOYEE RELATIONSHIP

Being friendly with those around you can be very effective, but not a mandatory trait of a good supervisor. In the context of performance, it is important to mention again that you should avoid becoming a close friend, or being related to, the people you supervise. It is a rare supervisor who can fairly evaluate relatives or friends.

Proceed carefully, or don't make friendships with coworkers for the same reason. The subordinate or coworker you haven't befriended will always feel at a disadvantage since you will focus on helping the friend.

Most of the time, a large majority of your employees want to do a good job, if for no other reason than to avoid a hassle. Do not develop your management style on the basis of the minority. It is important to note that if the majority of your team is not performing up to standard, and most of them want to do a good job, then you, as their supervisor, are not doing *your* job. You must be the teacher and mentor.

Note that there is little incentive for an hourly employee to think outside the box. Often they can be seen standing around idle waiting for instructions when a glitch has developed in a project. There is usually more risk of their being criticized for leaving the job in search of another job or an answer, than staying put. Again, a well described alternative job, or reaction to a potential complication solves this problem.

A manager, at any level, is responsible for the outcome of the team(s) supervised. As such, the manager must have a set of indicators that quickly identify if the team(s) managed is performing up to standard. Good managers don't micromanage. However, good managers don't let their subordinates make costly or dangerous mistakes all for the sake of avoiding micromanaging. If you know a subordinate supervisor is new to a position, and the supervisor is weak in an area, watch and help him or her until you are sure he or she has gained adequate experience.

If you find you are right and another individual or team is wrong, give the other person a way out. Try to find a way for that person to save face, and you will resolve the problem without developing an enemy. Something as simple as announcing that they were working with inaccurate data can eliminate bad feelings, while getting the job done more efficiently. No one likes to be caught in an error, so try to correct it without being confrontational. Obviously, chronic errors must be dealt with head-on.

Try to Avoid Supervising Friends

There is no such thing—or at least it is a very rare thing—as a complete friend in business, especially in the upper levels of management. The person you feel comfortable talking to about interpersonal issues may not be reliable in the future. Being friendly is good, but know that everything you say to people could become public knowledge—so, be careful. Friendships at upper management levels are about as secure and private as emails and social media.

Always keep in mind that others' motives and directions are not always what they seem to be…

I was involved with one operation working with a base material that had a unique way of changing color over time. As a result, over the years, the plant personnel had developed a normally adequate method that compensated for that unique behavior. Unfortunately, it required purposely entering incorrect data into the daily quality reports because their experience indicated the product would move into specification by the time it reached the customer. On one occasion, the wrong base material was used, and a complaint ensued. Once the practice was identified at a corporate level because of a quality complaint, heads had to roll. Despite several people in the organization, local and corporate, knowing of the practice, only one lower level manager was terminated; with several of his "friends" denying knowledge.

You cannot expect your "friends" to put their livelihood on the line to protect yours, and they can't expect you to do it for them.

SECTION III

DIG DEEPER:
COMMUNICATING

This section addresses communication and the bridge between management and team.

A key to keeping open communications with your subordinates is making sure they don't feel their job is on the line each time they talk to you.

Roof bolting Jumbo in an underground mine.

CHAPTER NINE

THE QUESTION

Properly using questions is probably the most vital tool that any manager has in his management toolbox.

- Ask questions of employees in a nonthreatening way:

Don't put them in the hot seat or give them a reason to fear losing their jobs. They will feel important that their opinion is valid to management, and they won't develop an "us against them" feeling.

- Ask the right questions:

Even if you know the answer (which you should), let them answer it.

You should care what they think; they are living it every day.

They will give you answers to problems you don't experience from your perspective. You may know what an answer to questions is, but you will get solutions that are from the point of view of the people who have to actually execute tasks. They have the right ideas; they just need to be asked for those ideas the right way.

As a manager, you are always looking for ways to save money and increase efficiency. If you were to walk up to the average hourly employee and ask "How do we make you 20% more efficient?" that question will be interpreted by the employee that he or she is not efficient enough and is going to be terminated. Most likely, you will not get an honest answer, and furthermore, you will get an employee who thinks his job is in jeopardy. Instead, figure out a way to ask that employee, who actually works down in the trenches, how you can make that job <u>easier</u> for them.

Your only goal is how to make the company better and more profitable. The hourly employee is only thinking about security of a paycheck and continued employment.

Don't Ask The Question if You Don't Want to Hear The Answer

Many times the boss knows how to solve a problem, but needs the team on board to get it done. The proper use of questions is the way to get there. By asking leading questions the boss can get the team members to come up with the correct (now their) answer, and will have a much stronger signoff by the team. Often, an even better solution will surface using this technique.

This is a roundtable style of collaborative management. You want input without your employees feeling threatened by the questions. They may have a sense of uneasiness when they actually have to commit to the answer, and you may be surprised at the number of people who don't like to do that. If you ask, "… is there any other way?" and the answer looks like everything's been covered and everyone is 100% sure, then you go with the collective decision. When everyone knows the boss is on board with the decision, the entire team will be as well.

If you ask someone for an opinion, let them give it to you *completely*. You don't want to find yourself inserting your (*i.e.*, the company's) opinions into the subordinate's answer before the opinion is complete. You asked for an opinion, wait for it. Learn to listen and be interested. If you interrupt or react by chastising the individual for an opinion that is undesirable, the next opinion you get will not be the true opinion. It will be what that person *thinks* you want to hear.

If that opinion doesn't match that of the company, then you, the supervisor, have been ineffective in transmitting the proper attitude. A positive takeaway for you would be awareness about how you can improve training your team. Seeking opinions and asking questions often becomes a teaching/learning opportunity for everyone.

The key is to ask the question, listen to the entire answer, and if it's not what you think it should be, then you go back to the drawing board and realize that it is not what you want your people to be thinking. You as their supervisor are doing something wrong.

If the subordinate's opinion reflects an unsafe attitude or activity, then you must take immediate action.

Listening or Hearing?

Many times, people use questions to show how smart they are versus actually hearing the answer. In many manufacturing processes, the people controlling the process may not completely understand the process but, through experience, know how to control it. They don't understand power or chemical reactions, but do know what to do if the product is not correct.

Don't ask people technical questions, that you know they can't answer correctly, just so you can show that person how smart you are by explaining the answer to your own question. If you do that, people will shut you down or shut you out. No one wants to feel stupid, especially in front of other team members. Validate their knowledge/contribution: ask them how they control that process, listen to the answer, and you may learn something about the process while gaining some respect in the process.

CHAPTER TEN

COMMUNICATING WITH YOUR EMPLOYEES

Communicating Change

I find change within a company to be a really fascinating aspect of management. Many, if not most, companies must evolve in order to stay current with their industries. When this process includes changing people versus equipment, it can be very difficult.

Almost all of us, when asked, admit we are not perfect. However, when pressed for details on their imperfections, most people stumble. Try blocking out a quiet thirty-minute period and study your own imperfections. Each of us may find some imperfections, but most of us will not recognize the degree to which those imperfections impact those around us.

Bottom line: everyone—subordinates included—will agree that change may be needed. However, self-examination will (often subconsciously) determine that, if everyone else changes to that individual's way of thinking, no more change will be needed. Each individual will downplay his imperfections and play up his strengths that fit the new changes.

When you need to communicate that behavioral change is needed, don't ever assume everyone will jump on board. Assume most won't truly agree to take action. You will have to carefully navigate personalities and identify what each individual needs to change within in order to facilitate the new company changes. Again, you must remember that you also need to change. Further on, we will discuss the value of each employee and the purpose of discipline if an employee has real difficulty with meeting the needs of change.

Infoclude

An Infoclude can be defined as "nothing flows through it." It's a play on a geological term: *aquiclude*: a barrier within the earth that restricts the flow of groundwater from one aquifer to another.

In other words, it is the differentiation between surface water and groundwater, and the thing that is excluding one from the other. Examples are a shale layer or a clay layer that won't allow the waters on the surface to migrate down to a lower level.

The flow of information between the hourly labor force and upper management is the same: *infoclude* means that information doesn't go up and doesn't come down.

Second-line supervisors can become an infoclude. They tend to rely on their experiences and, in their minds or by instinct, feel more secure because only they possess that knowledge. There is a large base of hourly employees in the average manufacturing facility—people actually doing the work—and they have a supervisor who relates more to them than to the company they work for. That supervisor brings the flow of information from the hourly employees to the second-line level of management, and vice-versa. The second-line supervisors, most of whom come from the ranks, tend to only let information flow back and forth as it suits their sense of security as opposed to company policy. If certain information makes them look weak, or if it looks like they might lose part of their responsibility, then they are most likely not going to share that information with their managers. If a general foreman (second-line) can figure out a way to have three supervisors on the shop floor instead of having four supervisors, he's probably not going to move that information up because as soon as they go to three, they won't need him.

This is an intuitive behavior and will not change, but it doesn't necessarily need to be changed. Controlling info is not the same as being in control. The manager must make sure the necessary information is flowing in <u>both</u> directions. When you are talking to a foreman on the shop floor, you must recognize the fact that everything that he sees is going to be in the perception and context of relating to himself and the hourly employees. He will protect himself and his experience, so ask questions that make him feel comfortable telling you what you need to know.

Conflict

There are always two sides to a conflict. Make sure you listen to and understand both sides before you make a decision. Too many times you will find yourself making a decision based on incomplete information and you end up backtracking. Do remember you are never dealing with people who think they are wrong or dumb, and to them, their side of the controversy is right.

Try to communicate only the things you know to your team. It is tempting to speculate to team members, but it is too risky. Often, team members will forget you prefaced a comment with "I think," and when it doesn't come to pass they feel you have lied. The team counts on you to *know* or to *find out*. You find out by asking, seeing, and understanding information from all of the involved stakeholders/team members. They are all valued parts of the solution (and may even <u>be</u> the problem).

CHAPTER ELEVEN

COMMUNICATING WITH YOUR BOSS

You have two responsibilities in management: doing the job you are being paid to do, and working for your boss. The idealists identify the boss as being the one responsible for a good working relationship but the fact is the subordinate bears the majority of the responsibility.

Often, bosses are promoted from within the team. While the new boss was a team member, his or her idiosyncrasies were just that, idiosyncrasies. However, once he or she becomes boss, those idiosyncrasies become supervisory flaws and become much more difficult for team members to deal with. Often these idiosyncrasies are not just annoying; they become detrimental and become a norm for the team.

Bosses are humans with human flaws—deal with it. In those rare cases where a boss is obviously destructive, the team should react by passing the information up the management structure.

Your boss is the main source of performance information about you to the next levels of upper management. As I described earlier, as bosses go, there are a few great, some good, and many bad. You must learn to deal with your boss so he or she will forward positive feedback about your performance. It is both naive and unrealistic to think everyone up the line of responsibility can see that you are a stellar performer if your boss is providing them negative feedback about you.

A boss will often promote an intellectually or structurally inferior second-string person over the first-string person.

This is because the second-string person is better at watching the boss's back; the boss feels more comfortable that the second-stringer has the boss's interests in mind whereas the first-stringer is more interested in self-promotion and being right. The boss's job is to look ahead and wants to be comfortable that the boss's behind is being watched. As difficult as it may seem, the thing you want to do is make your boss, even if the boss is flawed, look good.

You must totally understand the criteria being used to judge your performance. When you first start your career, your tasks and skills are well defined. As you move up within an organization, your original skills become less important and new manager skills become more important. For example, you just got promoted from a first-line to second-line supervisor of a manufacturer. Do not make the mistake of assuming that your boss is judging your ability to produce a product (something you are good at) when he or she is in reality now judging you on your ability to sell your ideas to the next layer of management.

Putting in lots of unpaid hours during routine operations (salaried employees) does not make you a good supervisor.

Usually, it's quite the opposite. You are either mismanaging your time or not delegating properly. Occasionally, it's a matter of enjoying the work environment more than the non-work environment. Whatever the reason, the extra hours do little to make you promotable.

In emergencies, or when dealing with projects, the opposite is true. In this case you have to put in the hours to get the job done. If you are overloaded, one of your key objectives is to get the help you need to get it done. Telling your boss that the project is behind because you didn't have time to take care of a key segment will register badly with the boss—the one person who controls your future.

Do Not Allow Your Boss to Be Blindsided

Keep the boss informed on risks, cost overruns, and other vital information without making it sound like you are asking for permission (to do your job). If you think an action you are planning may get a negative reaction from the team, let your boss know, as well as the reasons why you are doing it. Don't wait until your operation is cited for an environmental issue to inform your boss there may be an issue. Avoid tattle-tailing and whistle blowing.

Present Solutions, Not Problems

Don't just take problems to the boss. Bosses don't want to be presented with problems. They want *solutions*. Identify the problem and present a solution. Through discussion, your answer may be modified or rejected, but you are not just presenting problems.

Don't be afraid to compliment a good suggestion from the boss. Being human, the boss likes being stroked too (don't overdo it though, and be guilty of brown-nosing).

Most bosses have several equally responsible team members. Often the responsibilities overlap (production/maintenance, electrical/mechanical) and when differences of opinion arise, the team members have two choices. Make the boss decide who is right or work out a solution and present the boss with the solution. The latter is by far the best method since the boss, over time, may well decide to balance the wins vs doing the right thing. Worse yet, the boss may decide one of you will always be wrong.

Bosses have their own problems to solve and don't need the extra burden of solving team members' problems.

CHAPTER TWELVE

COMMUNICATING PROCESS: THE EASY WAY

Built-in controls (think speed limits) and standards for best/safest practices are very necessary. One of the simplest and most effective ways to improve environmental protocols, quality/maintenance programs, and safety is to make the right way the easiest way. Make the job easy and, coincidentally, safe.

Examples:

Environmental Protocol

A storm drain must be checked routinely to make sure it is clear and easily accessible. Give the inspector(s) easy access, and inspections will get done all the time. Make the inspector walk a mile through brambles and briars, and, at some point, the inspection will not get done.

If you have to go dig a ditch out every two or three hours to keep the water flowing in the right direction, eventually somebody's not going to do it. If you make it so the ditch is automatically self-flushing, and you know everything is designed around the safety of the water flow, then it can't get stopped up and it takes care of itself. Putting a machine or process in place to make the job easy will get the job done.

Quality/Maintenance

A conveyor belt underneath a crusher needs to be greased routinely, but the lubrication point is not easily accessible. The maintenance person must crawl down underneath it in the dark, get down on the floor, and get totally grimy scooting under the equipment. It is a difficult task, and even though it's the right thing to do and the maintenance personnel are getting paid to do it, it will not get done nearly as reliably as one with easy access from a standing position. It will get missed routinely, and either forgotten or put off for the next shift to handle. The conveyer belt will eventually break down and be difficult to replace, costing time and ultimately money. Put an extension on the point so the required work gets completed in an easier way, and the equipment continues to be properly maintained. With the fitting out in the open and visible, everyone that passes can see if it has been properly lubricated.

Safety

Imagine a job site that requires people to work on both sides of a pit. There is a safe walkway around that pit, but people have to climb a bunch of stairs and walk a long distance to get to the other side. However, there is a narrow beam across the pit that is easy to cross, but unsafe to use. Eventually, someone who is lazy or in a hurry will use the beam and potentially have an accident. Make the beam the safe way, or drop in a walkway instead of the beam, and the problem is solved.

When I graduated from college in 1965, I was one of those people who went into safe mining kicking and screaming. At the time, mining was considered to be a rough, tough business; a manly business, in which big strong guys didn't need to be supervised from a safety perspective. My job was to tell them how to do it safely, but it was their choice if they did it safely or not. I had to go through a major transition myself, mentally. It was really hard for me to get through my head that you have to keep after people to make things safer. Regardless of how many times you tell them, it was still the responsibility of the supervisor to make sure that employees were safe.

I graduated with a mining engineer who transferred to my division. I was the master mechanic at the time, and he was the safety director. I can remember vividly, he and I were standing at the elevator where everybody went underground. All work had ceased as the miners refused to get on that elevator because it was unsafe. As master mechanic, I was responsible for its repair, and my colleague was called in. It turned out that the problem was a redundant safety measure, but it wasn't functioning. The entire mine shut down because nobody would ride on this cage. He and I were going nose to nose. He was saying, "Fix it." I was saying it was redundant and the miners should ride it. At one point I asked him how he would fix it, because he also was a mining engineer.

He said to me quite simply, "It is not my job. It is your job to fix it. It is my job to declare it unsafe."

He was right, of course. It took me years to get that logic into my head, because he was a mining engineer, and I thought that he and I together should be able to solve the problem, or deem it unsolvable. But I was, as the master mechanic, the one responsible for solving and fixing the problem.

As a supervisor, you MUST feel totally responsible for the team even when you are not present. The supervisor is responsible for developing the team attitude so that when that team is working independently, it is second nature to them. If an employee is hurt, it is partly the supervisor's fault because that employee wasn't adequately trained to avoid the cause of the accident. Don't back away from this responsibility just because it requires repetition and confrontation.

In each of these examples, the common thread is recognizing the importance of the task being easy to accomplish. The operator will naturally want to find an easier way to do a job. Better access or machinery placed so the easiest way is also the safe way. It is better to make that easier way a company mandated and properly set up system, than to have the operator rig up a shortcut that is unsafe.

With all of these disciplines, you absolutely cannot "do as I say not as I do." You are compromising yourself, and more importantly, your team will pick up this attitude. Again, you are responsible for the team while at work even when they are not with you. They will take risks—just like you—and eventually those risks will catch up to them. This is a particularly difficult concept for many supervisors, particularly if the supervisor thinks he is being judged by his superiors on production as opposed to good practices.

SECTION IV

TEAM

Building your team means getting the most out of the people whom you manage, and most honestly, finding their weaknesses.

Part of a large team of people who make a mine operation run.

CHAPTER THIRTEEN

TEAM BUILDING & MANAGEMENT

I use the word "team" for lack of a better term. I don't like the reference to sports, and don't intend the use of the term in that way. I have always believed that running a department or a company is nothing like running a sports team. I understand that usage but have always tried to stay away from it in my management style. As a manager, you will have a "team" of people that you are managing. I believe the similarity ends there.

Do Not Make Your Team in Your Own Image

When assembling a team of department heads, don't clone yourself; don't hire people who are just like you. In a corporation, you absolutely do not want everyone in the organization to be the same type of people. An autocratic-type CEO will end up with those same types of people in most of the department head positions. An HR person has to be an HR person, not a bottom-line capitalist-type person in an HR position. You need to hire people for their expertise and put them in those expert positions. If you have people who not only bring an area of expertise but also have broader talents, move those types of people up through your organization. Just don't have yourself sitting down looking at yourself at the table.

Each one of us has strengths and weaknesses. Don't staff a team with people with the same strengths and weaknesses. Some employees have good analytical skills and weak people skills, while others are exactly the opposite. The same is true for people-oriented styles where autocrats are avoided at all costs. One manager can't and shouldn't do the things that another department manager does well and vice versa. Teams need good balance, and the ability to bend and give flexibility. That enables sustainability and productive, effective systems.

Companies that I have worked for promoted only people who presented themselves well. They should have had one or two who presented themselves well, but they still needed to have people that were skilled at making and improving their products, costs, and process. In these cases, the top dogs in a manufacturing company didn't have any manufacturing instincts whatsoever. How does something like that happen? They presented themselves well to upper management, and happened to work in a corporation that was more or less coasting on its product pricing success, but not really growing or improving. They had people at the plant level who knew how to run their processes reasonably well, not the best, but reasonably well, so things went on as normal. The business self-corrected and basically took care of itself. In other words, things just kind of leveled off. There was really no incentive to take the cost side of the business to the next level of success. I don't necessarily think it was because they were complacent or didn't care. I think it was more a matter of "they don't know what they don't know," and one thing they didn't know was they were missing opportunities because of things running reasonably well and they thought that's all there was to it.

A curious note is the observation that these same people who present themselves will also have "college bowl" memories. These are people whose memories approach photographic, and facts are immediately on the tips of their tongues. People like me, who are not blessed with this attribute, have to work harder to compete on the same platform; but it is doable.

Sometimes as the supervisor, you must learn to deal with the hand (team) you are dealt. Because you are the boss, you are probably "gifted" with more than the average knowledge of the work being done. Each team member does his own valuable *part* of the work, but the supervisor knows, or at least understands, most of the elements involved in the overall job. Your team does not know all that you know, so do not presume that all the members of your team have the same level of "gifts." Everyone has their own "gifts," and the supervisor must manage all off those gifts.

For example, a team member who is slow with mathematics is usually not slow by choice, but by aptitude. This is simply the nature of the beast. Being good at mathematics is a gift, not a given. Find ways to capitalize on each team member's gift(s) and work with each team member to strengthen his or her weaknesses. Do not expect all team members to be as smart as you, but be happy to have the ones who are, because they are the ones that will make you promotable. Acknowledge and nurture the gifts, and the employee will be more likely to develop other gifts and will key in on and maximize his or her strengths.

As for the person who is typically weak in arithmetic, make sure that there's a controller there working with him or her to make sure that weakness in arithmetic is not hurting the overall performance. You'll hopefully improve that person's weakness at least to an acceptable level, but if it ultimately gets to the point that it becomes detrimental to his or her performance, you may eventually have to reposition or terminate that person.

Use other people's strengths to cover other people's weaknesses and don't expect everybody to be great at everything. If you do see that there is the one person who is "broad brush"—having a variety of strengths—and does not possess outstanding weaknesses, that is the person you want to promote and move up in the organization. As for the rest of your people, just make sure that their weaknesses are covered by somebody else.

This goes back to the idea that you don't want to "clone" yourself. Make sure that you have people who are good at arithmetic, excel in human interaction skills, and are intuitive about blowing things up (in the mining world)!

When I walked into a manufacturing environment where the staff was already in place and established, I would be able to find all the strengths of the people that were there fairly quickly, and capitalize on those strengths. If I had a staff that was producing at a certain level, generally speaking, I could take that same staff and move their level of performance up just by working with them on their strengths and trying to cover on the weaknesses. Many managers just do a mass, general type of team building to make everybody kind of semi-strong in their weaknesses, but not really capitalize on their strengths.

A weakness of mine is that I will work with people longer than most upper managers will...most upper managers will hire somebody into position and say, "come across or walk." Time is money, and if those position people don't adapt and improve, they don't work at that company very long.

I will work with the team to get the absolute max out of those people, instead of getting rid of individuals and finding somebody else. It's kind of the old adage of be careful what you ask for: with the current person, you are dealing with someone you know. If you replace that person, you're dealing with an unknown in the replacement. I always want to absolutely maximize the team, and I think I was very good at being able to get the best and most out of them.

Personnel

Do not team up a good performer with a weaker one. You will invariably drag down the attitude and performance of the good performer. Over time you will not come out with average performance; it will not average out, it will be unacceptable performance. Allow the good one(s) to perform at his or her own level and concentrate your training and teaching on the weaker performer. The net outcome will be an overall increase in performance.

Telegraph Your Moves

The best way to get a team behind a project is to have it be their idea. A good team leader will frequently know the right answer or what was thought to be the right answer, as well as one that may not be best, and should be open with no preconceived outcomes (he or she was made manager because of this ability). Through carefully crafted questions and discussion, he or she can coax the right answer out of the team. When it's the team's idea, they will automatically sign off on it. This can be more difficult than it sounds simply because it is difficult for managers not to claim responsibility for success of an idea—especially if the idea originated from the manager. This is also a very valuable tool in meetings.

Most times, telegraphing your moves is a vital part of building teams. If you decide to change an old practice that is non-productive, don't just do it overnight. Lead up to it, discuss the need for the change with the team, listen to their input, and then enact the change. It takes at least two weeks to develop a "habit." It is the same with instituting changes in procedures or practices.

About the only time you don't want to telegraph your moves is when you don't have control of the move you are planning. If the company is thinking about bonuses, don't talk about it until you are putting the bonus check in the employees' hands. If you are planning to change your style based on their input, don't telegraph it—just begin the change, then monitor and adjust if needed during the progress. Again, in most cases telegraph your moves.

Everyone is Replaceable

Do not overestimate your own importance. Everyone—*absolutely everyone*—is replaceable. It's quite amazing to most people who think they are irreplaceable how the organization continues when they're gone. To think that when you quit, the company will suffer in any way is so naive and self-centered because in most cases that company was here long before you were, and it will be here long after you're gone. There might be a glitch in there, or someone may lose track of some paperwork or something, but the operation will not fold up due to the loss of any one employee. It will happen with every organization, some key superintendent quits and the rest of the management team has to step up and the job gets done until a new supervisor is hired. The team will fill the void until the void is filled. They might encounter some glitches along the way, but the company will still survive. The management team covers until they get somebody in permanently.

When I left my last job in Canada, there was a fond farewell, but they slipped somebody in behind me almost immediately. He might have had a different way of doing it, but he got the job done effectively. I can't think of any example my career history that when somebody left, the company actually suffered irreparably.

Discipline

Discipline should be an opportunity to change an employee's behavior and an opportunity for that employee to learn—not a way to get rid of that employee. Especially in today's world, a lot of money and time are spent training employees to do a safe and competent job. Your company has invested time and money into the workforce by way of training on equipment, procedures, and safety. Don't throw that investment away until you have exhausted all training and disciplinary options. Hundreds of hours and tens of thousands of dollars are invested in training each employee *every year* just to keep current with the law, let alone how to run the equipment they work on. Just because somebody is not performing the way you want them to, it is not necessarily the smartest move to just find a way to fire him or her.

Never discipline an employee in front of others unless the violation is for a safety issue. You have lost a majority of your words and disciplinary efforts if the employee is defending himself in front of his peers. Tempers then become the issue, not the actions requiring the discipline. Maintain a respectful relationship with your team members.

For example, if you suspect an employee may be sleeping on shift, start with re-explaining the policy to the entire team. Be careful and mindful so innocent team members don't feel they are being yelled at when in fact they are doing nothing wrong; the team will probably know who the offender is. Often, sleeping on the job is a serious offense resulting in termination. You may suspect a relatively poor performer is guilty—but you may be wrong. Your objective should be to stop the sleeping on the job, not to fire an employee. By re-explaining the policy and then checking for sleeping, you are most likely to stop the practice versus potentially firing an otherwise good, well-trained employee. A good manager must react consistently and immediately whenever a violation of policy, especially safety, is observed.

As stated earlier, disciplining a friend or family member is extremely difficult. Often discipline is appropriate, but may be minimized or not carried out because you know the issues and background of the individual, and you will tend to overlook their shortfalls. Many organizations forbid fraternizing in policy statements.

Improving Employee Performance

Try to counsel an employee as they begin to develop unacceptable behavior; find a way to work with the employee on those kinds of issues before they become a disciplinary issue. Many labor contracts have a very effective three-step disciplinary action that consists of the verbal process, written process, and if insufficient progress, termination. You have to put people on notice and explain specifically what they're doing wrong in terms of violating a particular function or responsibility. A similar process works well with the staff. The most difficult part is defining the employee's weaknesses and making sure that the needed corrections are well defined and measurable. If an employee is not filling out paperwork appropriately (for example, weekly reports), review the shortcoming immediately—don't wait for a month and then observe that the employee missed four reports.

If you feel that the employee actually has the capability to become the employee that the company is looking for, that person will know that you and the company find value in him or her, and this process is the venue to work through together to help get him or her there. In my experience, if you have an employee who is basically not a fit with the company or team and his or her weaknesses are so dominant that he or she will never get through the improvement program, generally that employee will leave before the end of the program. You won't have to terminate the employee because he or she will recognize the lack of fit and will leave.

Crisis Management

Do not make the mistake of trying to fix blame during a crisis. In many companies, blame is demanded from higher up. We watch this happen all the time on television when commentators start searching for someone to blame long before a problem is resolved. That may work for them, but it has no place in the work environment. You need all hands to solve a problem; you don't want your team covering themselves because you are trying to affix blame as opposed to solving the problem. Once the problem is solved and all the facts are available then seek ways to avoid a similar problem *without* affixing blame, if possible. Although it is necessary to find the cause, instead of looking for a place to lay blame, look at it as a learning experience for you and the team as a whole. Once all the facts are available, affix blame, if necessary, but don't start out with blame in mind.

During a crisis, be upbeat. People will respond much better and come up with quality solutions when they are working in a positive atmosphere. You are all in it together, so involve your team by asking them how to fix the problem.

CHAPTER FOURTEEN

THE PROMOTABLE PERSON

This chapter covers your promotability,
and recognizes the promotability of those you supervise.

The most promotable person is the one who sees opportunity. That person will also have the insight to look ahead and see what impact a planned action will have downstream. You don't want to sell your boss on an idea, let him or her champion the idea, then at some later point say, "Whoops, it won't work because of something you didn't think of." On the other hand, the less promotable person will not make the proposal for fear of making a mistake. The promotable person will vet the proposal thoroughly and present it in a timely fashion.

Demonstrate your value to the organization. Sometimes an idea bombs, and the outcome of that risk will depend a lot on the nature of the boss and the company. Make sure you understand this before taking the risk.

The promotable person will always make sure the time being spent on a problem is appropriate to the size or impact of the problem being solved. Finding the cheapest place to change a tire doesn't come close to the cost of having your delivery truck down while you're searching for the cheapest tire store. The promotable person recognizes what the boss or company considers critical and makes sure he or she is spending the time necessary to meet their criteria not spending time working on non-critical issues. This relates directly to perception; what you think the company priorities *should be* is quite irrelevant if it is not in line with the actual company priorities.

The expression "no such thing as a free lunch" is appropriate with respect to promotion. As a person moves up the corporate ladder, he or she has to pay a price. The higher you are in the organization, the less you can delegate key decisions and activities. You need to provide opportunities to others you manage and support them. You will have fewer people with whom you can talk and brainstorm. People who were once your peers now are your subordinates, and will definitely treat you differently now that you control their future versus being a part of it. Some of them will be willing to use that past relationship with you to their advantage for personal gain, so you need to set boundaries and expectations right away. Very often, promotions require relocating to the job, away from family and friends.

There are other prices that many otherwise qualified people are *not* willing to pay for promotion in addition to those mentioned earlier. Many do not want to make subordinates do the right thing or get in the face of a subordinate. They don't want the stigma of "doing anything to get ahead," or don't want to be held responsible for mistakes. The unfortunate thing is that when they are promoted or put in situations they aren't comfortable with or equipped to handle, they do not recognize their unwillingness to pay the prices and are quick to blame someone or company politics for their lack of progress.

Other aspects of the promotable person include:

Command Presence

A "command presence" is a very important upper-management attribute. There are some people that can walk into a room and people will automatically pay attention to them, just by the way they look. You will never see people moving a long way up an organization that don't have, or can't work on, commanding presence

In other words, if you walk into the room as the manager of a plant, everybody in the room *has* to recognize that you are the manager. Some people just can't get there; they can't or won't look people in the eye, or they are quiet and super reserved. Very seldom do we see people lacking a command presence make it to upper management levels. People like me, who do not have a physical "command presence" need a different way to gain presence, such as through conversation and asking intelligent questions. If you're neither of the above, then it's hard to move up through an organization. People who have "it" take a significant step in the right direction.

Some commanding presence qualities:
- How they look
- How they conduct themselves
- They will look people in the eye
- If quiet/reserved, it is a confident, commanding kind

Public Speaking

I knew right from the get-go that I was very uncomfortable speaking in public—sometimes to the point where I was sick to my stomach. I had to force myself to go into it because I knew darn well where I wanted to go with my career, I had to be able to function in public speaking mode. At one job, I was going to board meetings, either as a board member or reporting to the board, seven times a year, and it still made me nervous to the point of not being able to sleep the night before. I'd have to force myself into doing it because I knew that I was not going to get very far in the executive level of a pretty decent-sized company if I couldn't stand up and speak.

SECTION V
CONTRACTS

*The best contract is one that has been drawn up
in the best interest of BOTH parties.*

Open pit mine, British Columbia, Canada.

CHAPTER FIFTEEN

THERE IS NO ADVANTAGE IN TAKING ADVANTAGE OF SOMEONE ELSE

A contract is similar to a speed limit on the highways. Without a speed limit, people will drive too fast. Without a contract, some managers will abuse their authority. With a contract, you don't have to waste time and energy disputing, compromising, and negotiating everything because the contract has done that.

The best contract is one that has been drawn up in the best interest of BOTH parties. Don't build things into a contract that can take advantage of the other company or the labor force. Make sure that the companies you contract with, or people working for you, have a good shot at making a living at it and that you don't take advantage of somebody.

If you have to haul your product to your customer, it is your responsibility as a manufacturer to carry that cost, because it is your material. If you can't survive at that cost, you don't need to be in business. If you know that the haulage is going to be super expensive, but create a contract that you know your hauler cannot profit from, and is going to have to accept some part of that haulage cost, that is just wrong, and moreover, it is crooked.

The same goes for building in and taking advantage of some sort of loophole in the labor contract. You are going to have an angry group of people who make up your workforce when you take advantage of that loophole. And when it is time to make a new contract with the workforce, those people will remember what you did to them, and you will have a lot of difficulty coming up with a contract that works in everyone's best interest.

Labor Contracts

A labor contract is just that: a contract. You as a supervisor may not agree with all the provisions of the contract, but you are obliged to adhere to it. You can't expect employees to abide by it if they are aware their supervisor doesn't do the best he or she can to both understand and abide by that contract. Too many times, supervisors will try to bend or outright violate the contract in an incorrect belief they are helping the company. Violating or undermining a contract should be considered a violation of company policy and dealt with accordingly.

For several years at a union operation, my nickname was "pig-pen" because I carried a tool pouch and, for years, I got dirty teaching people how to get things fixed. I always did this as a training mode with a union employee present. Not once, despite being watched closely by the union, did I receive a grievance because I was always very careful to work within the letter and spirit of the contract.

Many managers think a labor contract is a burden they would not have in a non-union plant. What you have and what you want rarely happen. In the case of several very large powerful unions, the contract is a major difficulty for management. However, most labor contracts are a good tool for both union employees and management. The contract defines how conflicts are to be handled, and by whom. A contract removes many personality issues by defining activities (especially in the realm of discipline) that otherwise could be considered sources of favoritism.

It is important to note that the contract also spells out what management can do, not just limitations. Too often, supervisors develop the attitude that the contract doesn't allow them to manage, thus they don't enforce the conditions of the contract. Many supervisors feel they can't get rid of chronically poor employees, while the contract carefully spells out the procedure(s) required to do just that. It's more work for the supervisor and often requires confrontation, but it's totally doable and it is not an option to disregard.

CHAPTER SIXTEEN

PAY WHAT IT IS GOING TO TAKE

Your company is building a manufacturing plant, and you contract a local haulage company to clear the area to build. You know that haulage company is going to have difficulty because they have to get off the road with their regular road trucks, which will tear up their trucks to get into your site. You sign a contract with them that says all of the cost of building a road on your site and/or maintaining their trucks is on their back not yours—which you know essentially means they have underbid that contract. All of a sudden you have a small company that is part of the community that has to go out of business because they agreed to a contract that you knew was not in their best interest.

Look at it from the standpoint that you know that you have to put in the road—and it is *your* road—and you want to have a contractor put it in and make his five or seven percent profit. Pay that price for it. Don't sit there and accept another contractor coming in with a significantly lower bid that you know will cause him to fail.

It may work out to your advantage at first, but if the contract results in losses that cause that business to shut down, not only has a local community lost an employer, but when it is time to find a new company to contract, those companies will learn from the mistakes you and the original company made on the first contract and will make the contract work only in their best interest, because now YOU are at a disadvantage, and they can exploit that.

*A company I worked for, prior to my going to Canada, always attempted to build vagueness into contracts. The purpose was to give the company opportunities to twist the contract in its favor—**after** the contract was signed. I was not responsible for those contracts, but I was responsible for the contracts when I was with the position I took in Canada. At that mining company, one of our mines was near the top of a mountain, and the snow season stretched from September to May and was measured in feet—not inches. The final access to the mine was a thirty-eight kilometer, single lane gravel road. We knew this was a very difficult haul of the materials we pulled out of that mine. Keeping the roads clear of the snow was also incredibly challenging. We realized that getting the mined material to its final destination would need a two-tiered approach. We worked not only with the haulage company but also with a local native group*

The native company was extremely skilled at operating road clearing equipment and keeping roads open in general. The first contract with the native group included equipment availability clauses and was based on annual average snowfall. While we were developing the new contract, we learned the native group was losing significant amounts of money in the high snow years, mainly because they did not have the best equipment for the task. We also learned they had great operating skills but poor business skills. We decided to fill this void in experience by crafting a contract that had us paying what it really cost to move the mountains of snow. Also, recognizing their equipment was undersized and old, we bought the equipment needed with a payback plan over the tenure of the contract. This resulted in exceptional care of the road, and most importantly, good will that carried over into many other dealings with that group.

The second contract was with a large, well-respected hauling company. They were contracted to haul our product down the mountain, then more than 150 kilometers on improved, paved roads, to the seaport. Over the first two years of the contract, this company had major difficulty with getting their costs down due to the extreme road and weather conditions. With one year left in our contract and absolutely no other possible haulers available (those other hauling companies all knew about the conditions and wouldn't even bid on this job), we had to react. We had our accountant go over their books (with their blessing, of course) to confirm they were losing money. Once we determined they, in fact, were losing significantly, we surprised them mightily. We paid them their losses and included a modest profit amounting to hundreds of thousands of dollars. They agreed to continue the haulage contract at the new rates, plus inflation, for the remaining life (five years) of the mine. Both of our companies were winners: the haul contactor continued to generate a profit, and our company saved a significant amount of money by not having to purchase equipment and train drivers; or not having to pay the huge tonnage rate expected if another contractor was found.

Now the rest of the story: As part of the deal with the haulage contractor, we mandated that they work with the native business group to maximize that group's participation in the hauling. We wanted no part in the negotiations but required that both companies sign and approve the contract. The native group had excellent drivers for the mountain road but lacked the number of licensed drivers to consistently haul on the improved highways. The final agreement involved native drivers for the highway portion of the haul and company drivers finishing the route to the port. Winners all around. We gained national recognition as a company that worked well with native groups as well as getting a solid haul contract for the life of the mine. The haul contractor received a consistent income; but more importantly, this was the first of its kind of contract in Canada, and it opened more opportunities for them in the future. The native group got more and steady work for their constituents.

If they hadn't bid on the job, we would have had to buy the equipment, which would have cost us millions of dollars. It was in our best interest to have the haulage company satisfied with the contract.

CONCLUSION

During my career, I spent a lot of time in my truck, driving between home and whatever mine I was working at the time. Most of my commute consisted of driving on long, lonely roads and highways which took me to remote, often desolate, middle-of-nowhere locations where the mines were. During the many years of those early morning and evening trips, I had plenty of time to think about, and over time develop and put in practice, my management philosophy. When I had a thought, I knew I needed to write it down immediately or I would lose it forever, and I had one of those little note pads on the steering wheel with a slot to hold a pen so I could jot down my ideas during my trip to and from my workplace. The results of those trips, those thoughts, and those notes are contained in these pages.

My style of management was to ask questions. This book started out with the thoughts and notes I jotted down, more often than not, with a question:

"Does this really make sense in the big picture of management?"

As I began to decipher and compile all of those years of notes into this book, one chapter for each concept or philosophy of management, I initially used the title "YOU," and designed it to engage the reader—the aspiring or experienced manager—to examine his or her own management philosophy from an internal perspective. The concept was—and is—that it all comes down to YOU. *Your* attitude and *your* big picture outlook of your job will determine and ultimately define your success; how you as a manager can impact the function of your operation, and how your actions impact your development. After I had put those pieces together, I decided I wanted to *dig deeper* to expand and expound on each of those concepts and philosophies with anecdotal accounts and experiences that were the actual inspirations to write down on that little note pad on the steering wheel.

Mountain mine operation, British Columbia, Canada.

ACKNOWLEDGMENTS

This book started with Brenda Parks in the early 1980's. Without her typing and editing skills, input, and dedication, this project would not have started.

Jeanne Leeck is the Director of Social Services at a local health care facility. Her recent enthusiasm and support for the book's content fueled my determination to have it published.

ABOUT THE AUTHORS

MICHAEL YOUNG

Mike was born in Kirkland Lake, Northern Ontario, in 1942. His family moved to the Toronto area when he was three years old and stayed in that area until 1953, when the family moved to Blind River, Ontario, where his father was made manager of the first of multiple uranium mines in the newly discovered Elliot Lake mining district. Mike spent the last three years of high school at a boarding school in Southern Ontario, returning home by train on holidays. He followed his father's footsteps to Michigan College of Mines (now Michigan Technological University) where he received, like his father, a Bachelor of Science degree in Mining Engineering in 1965.

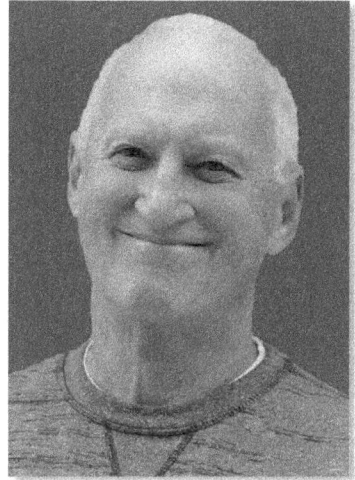

Mike married in 1964, and upon graduation, he and his wife moved to an underground mining operation in Virginia, where all three of their children were born. While in Virginia, he attended graduate school at Virginia Polytechnic Institute, where he earned his Masters of Engineering degree.

In 1970 the family moved to Missouri to one of the major new underground lead/zinc mines in the "New Lead Belt." This mining district pioneered some of the most important underground mining technologies of the time. He started as the Production Engineer for the underground mine operations, and left in 1985 as the General Manager.

In 1985 he took a headquarters position in New Jersey (eventually transferring to Maryland) as Director of Manufacturing for a mining/manufacturing company that operated four surface mines with associated manufacturing facilities.

In 1995 he took the position of Vice President of Operations with the Canadian division of a major US gold mining company. He and his wife moved to northern Washington State, and he commuted to his office in Vancouver, British Columbia, Canada. He was responsible for four underground mines in British Columbia and Ontario, and was on three mining company boards.

In 1998 he resigned from that position, and, as a result of his wife's ill health, decided to not pursue another full-time position. He now resides in central Wisconsin, and is currently consulting in the mining industry.

MICHAEL NICLOY

Michael is a team writer and publisher for Reji Laberje Writing and Publishing. He lives with his wife, Angela, son Liam MK, and dog Quincy in Mukwonago, Wisconsin; where they are allowed to live by their cat, Sasha.